REFLECTIONS

REFLECTIONS

In Search of God

Leo G. Morin

Edited and with a Preface by

Gregory T. Morin

Revelum Press

Cheyenne, WY

Revelum Press • Cheyenne, Wyoming
Second Edition

Cover Design & Interior Formatting by Gregory T. Morin
Edited by Gregory T. Morin

Text font is Adobe Caslon

Second Edition

ISBN Paperback	979-8-9953681-2-0
ISBN Ebook	979-8-9953681-1-3

I passed from a desperation to extricate myself from the grime of desolate poverty to a longing to linger where the Lord physically touched me and looked me in the face

–Leo G. Morin

Contents

Foreword

LEO WAS A FRIEND. He was a gentle spirit. He was a fellow Jesuit seminarian brother, whose life moved in a different direction, but who I can confidently say found the love of the Lord or as he put it "...the difference between God and the idea of God" when he accepted my invitation to visit Jamaica. I had initiated a Brotherhood of men, Missionaries of the Poor (MOP), who was answering the call of the gospel to serve the poor. While visiting one of the homes for the poor Leo tells us of this epiphany when Garth, one of the young residents who was non-verbal, took his hand as he walked through "Good Shepherd", one of our MOP homes.

As I remember Leo, I know the Lord uses us to lift up others, and it has been my joy and comfort to know that even though we did not see each other in the recent years, he felt that love during his many visits caring for the residents in our homes. I recall with warmth and affection Leo's deep faith which I see has flowed to his second and third generation.

You have run your race, my friend, through the trials and disappointments, while taking in the joy offered by God's people. You, Leo, are indeed accepted as an Associate of the Missionaries of the Poor.

May readers find hope and realize the joy that the Lord offers in this your first and only publication!

Fr. Richard Ho Lung
Founder
Missionaries of the Poor
Kingston, Jamaica
March 2026

Foreword

AFTER SPENDING SEVERAL years eating breakfast on Thursdays with Leo, I have come to love him for his faith and compassion. We have hauled horses together, talked religion, business and politics together, looked for restaurants together, laughed together and cried together. But most of all we shared our faith and convictions.

What began as a meeting of two souls seeking for counsel, developed into a friendship for which there were no words. When people would see us together, they would inquire as to whether we were brothers. There seemed to be something that was beyond two men meeting to eat breakfast. In December 1997 there came into this life a little boy that bonded us even closer. It is appropriate that his name was Nicklas Morin. He became a part of our breakfast meetings and at first consumed only the bottle that was sent with him. Later he would be a partaker of our sausage, bacon, eggs and pancakes. We were Pop-Pop Leo and Pop-Pop Paul. Joining with us in our gatherings was Nick's dad Gregory. This trio of men was symbolized in Nicklas Gregory Morin. As he moved from each of us selecting what he wanted and needed, so we each ate of the spiritual food the others had to offer.

I believe I know and understand his desire in writing this book. Leo has seen the good side of life and he has seen the low side of life. Through all the good and the bad he has seen the one element that gives meaning to life. It can be summed up in one word, GOD. He has seen God in the faces of the disadvantaged people of Jamaica. He has seen God in the faces of the people who tended to the disadvantaged people of Jamaica. He has seen God in those who reached out in thankfulness as he tended to those who have truly suffered the plagues that can come upon this fleshly body in which we exist.

Leo learned more about God tending to the deformed people of Jamaica than all the years he spent studying to be a Priest or listening to the Sunday homilies. Because we can learn more of God and his compassion for us when we show compassion to others, it is his hope that in this book he can direct the eyes of the reader away from the cares of this life to the one sure element that never changes and that is God.

I understand the frustration of knowing that someday we will depart from this life and our concern and desires for our children, grandchildren and those we love will be silenced. We wonder what the future will hold for them and the direction they will take. Our desire is to somehow light a candle that will shine in the darkness to direct them back into the course of this life that is sure and the benefits eternal.

My prayer is that those who read this book will be able to see what Leo has seen.

Take a walk with Jesus
amongst those who are
maimed and deformed

Take a walk with Jesus
to lift up those
whose bodies are forlorn

Take a walk with Jesus
as he sought to heal
those who had been scorned

Take a walk with Jesus
shine the light of day
to the maimed and deformed

My one regret is that Leo and I were not able to take this walk together.

Gene Paul Nicklas
Lilburn, Georgia
February 2001

Preface

I WAS IMBUED FROM CHILDHOOD in traditionalist Roman Catholicism. Everything about the Church was accepted without question. The rosary was prayed at home, Mass attended religiously, Catholic school from first grade, through high school, through college. While I had a brief teen-age religious rebellion, religion was clearly pivotal in my life. Most of this was heavily burdened with pre-Vatican II practices. I was obsessed with the intellectual spirituality of the Jesuits and joined them, spending about six years of my young adulthood living scrupulously the life of poverty, chastity, and obedience.

After experiencing much disillusionment and extreme loneliness, as much from my own failures as the Jesuits' and the Church's, I reluctantly left the Jesuits, feeling for many years thereafter that I had given up on God. The feeling eventually became reality, and I drifted in and out of the Church for years, punctuated with my share of raising three children. Clearly, the idea of God occupied a consuming role in my life. But I was by inclination and education a man of science. Intellectual integrity was equally consuming. That God and science could be at odds was an uncomfortable and unacceptable position for me and I was never prepared or willing to give up either. Much of my mindful life was obsessed with finding God in science, philosophy, and theology.

My journey in search of God took an unexpected turn after 57 years when, in the eyes of an epileptic Jamaican boy, I serendipitously discovered the difference between God and the idea of God and realized that Faith is not the acceptance of doctrine. My sense of God's presence in this search is so pervasive and my perspective on it so personal that I think it would be selfish not to share it with others, particularly my children and grandchildren, for whom this book is written, but also anyone troubled by the disturbances of Faith. The pressing urgency to share this search appreciates as my Faith finds itself in the ultimate and only real test of its integrity: approaching certain death by pancreatic carcinoma.

Reflections in search of God. I have chosen my words judiciously. I use "reflections" in the Pauline sense (1 Cor 13:12: Now we see but a poor reflection as in a mirror; then we shall see face to face.) and in its poetic sense of mental concentration or consideration. These reflections are at once tools of exploration in search of God and the distillations of that search. "Search" reinforces the Pauline anticipation of "then we shall see face to face." These reflections are personal meditations and are not meant to represent a cohesive intellectual apology for Christianity, Catholicity, or even a personal spiritual identity.

I am fully honest and open with my perspective and opinions. I do this for integrity, not to offend. At times, this may be politically incorrect and even Catholically incorrect.

Leo G. Morin
Madison, Georgia
February 2001

Editors Preface

TO THE READER I must first and foremost request forgiveness. My father, the author Leo Morin, passed away in March 2001 from pancreatic cancer. Near the end he asked that I assemble his manuscript for this book and have it published as an honest to God real book. I always intended to do so but as they say, life gets in the way. It seemed a monumental task, particularly considering the state of the publishing world circa early 2000-2010 where it was largely dominated by legacy publishing houses. I had no idea where to begin. But we now live in a glorious age where, with the help of numerous companies, anyone can publish their own book with only a few mouse clicks. I was out of excuses, so I am finally realizing my father's wish.

Because of his declining health in his final year many sections are not complete (many only a paragraph), so I beg once more the reader's forgiveness for the brevity of such sections. All words are his own. I have exercised the utmost restraint in any sort of rewording, with most edits being merely typographical and grammatical emendations. No AI was used to review or correct any text so any grammatical or typographical errors are mine alone.

Reflections: In Search of God is a selection of short essays that primarily contemplate what faith in God actually means. In the final years of his life, Leo experienced a profound spiritual transformation during mission work in Jamaica. These experiences broke through the barrier of his scientifically inclined mind leaving a heart transformed by an understanding of the difference between the idea of faith in God and actual faith in God. His views and opinions are those of a devout Catholic with the background of a Jesuit seminarian. However, these essays are not an apologia for Catholicism or the Church; they are based on the lived experience of a Catholic on a journey through a childhood grounded in the faith, young adulthood in seminary, the changes wrought by Vatican II, and eventually family and fatherhood. Leo wrote these essays in 2000 during the last year of his life. His final wish and hope was that his experience and words might influence others toward a deeper understanding of their faith in God.

My sincerest hope is that this tome brings the reader to the "reflections" my father intended and that perhaps it elicits a more perfect union and faith in God. On a personal note, I am pleased that this book is being published coincident with the baptism and confirmation of my youngest son, Zachary Leo Morin. At age 24 he has found the very faith my father writes of and that sadly has eluded his parents. Perhaps someday.

Gregory Morin
Cheyenne, Wyoming
March 2026

PART 1

THE PHILOSOPHY OF FAITH

In the Beginning

In the beginning was the Word... and the Word was God.
–John 1:1

SEVERAL YEARS AGO, Fr. Richard HoLung of Jamaica visited my parish and invited those there to heed the message of the gospel to go among the poor and the sick, not to do so by sending one's money for someone else to take our place, but to go ourselves. Everything in me said "NO! Don't even think of it!" But somewhere in me something kept asking, "Is the gospel real? Is the message real? Or is it just polite inconsequential piety?" I had known Richard years earlier when we were both Jesuits. He had left and founded the Missionaries of the Poor. I had married and raised three children and drifted in and out of the Church too many times. I went.

Upon arriving in Kingston, Jamaica, painfully, I recognized I was in a third-world country and that I had made a big mistake. Within minutes of visiting the centers where we were to work, I was terrified and repulsed by it all and I could think only of where to wash my hands each time I was touched and how to get on the earliest plane out. At the same time, I was embarrassed by myself and embarrassed to let anyone know how I felt.

Shortly after, at a shelter called *The Good Shepherd*, a young man, a boy, actually (Garth was his name) epileptic and retarded, never speaking, took me by the hand and would not let me go. He looked into my eyes, and I in his, and I suddenly realized I was looking into the Lord's eyes, and he was holding my hand. My eyes were seeing what they had never seen before. I was experiencing the personal relationship with the Lord that had eluded me for so long. Without speaking, Garth gave graphic testimony to the Word. I passed from a desperation to extricate myself from the grime of desolate poverty to a longing to linger where the Lord physically touched me and looked me in the face. Leaving at the end of the week, which I first thought could not come soon enough, had come much too soon.

I returned to Good Shepherd by myself the following spring and several times after with my Church group. In all my returns, the experience of the Lord's presence grew more intense. That is until my most recent trip. Upon visiting a shelter called *The Lord's Place* (most appropriately, it turns out!) I had become paralyzed with fear and anger with God at the sight and smell of suffering children and could not bring myself to function there. I resolved to deal with it. I made friends with Julian, a young boy with cerebral palsy. I fed Julian, I walked Julian, I changed and bathed Julian. Julian has a contagious smile. Until then, I had seen the Lord in others. Julian was the Lord's way of letting me see Him in myself.

After half a century of Christian living, it took a boy, both physically and mentally hampered, a boy who never spoke a word, to take me by the hand and look into my eyes, to gift me with the awareness, the experience to my very being of God's loving presence. This boy had showed me unconditional love and I knew I was with God, that God was holding my hand and that I was looking into God's eyes. This was the gift of the experience of faith. No longer was faith a theological abstraction. This had nothing to do with doctrine. This boy found his way deep into my heart where no one had been before and he brought Christ with him. I had discovered the difference between God and the idea of God. I had discovered Faith. I had discovered the Incarnation. I had discovered that I too could be God to others. I had discovered Eucharist. I had looked upon God's face. I could never again be the same.

still unspoken joy
hushed grief of affliction
echo to God's pain

gleam of radiance
smitten by infirmity
mirror to God's love

The arid erudition and cerebral questions of philosophy and theology are important because convictions of improbability must be defused, but they do not bring us to Faith. Instead, Faith thrives in the fertile heart that is open to the refuse of humanity: Blessed are the poor in spirit. God is most visible, most palpable in the presence of suffering. It is in the human condition that, with increasing comfort, God becomes increasingly invisible. That is because separation is the root of pain and our pain is a reflection of God's own pain. Pain speaks to us forcibly of our longing not to be separated from God, and, more so, of God's longing to be one with us. To be poor in spirit is to be aware of separation from God. None of the beatitudes are possible without the first.

"O' come Emmanuel and ransom captive Israel in lonely exile."

No matter how grim the situation, always remember that salvation comes from faith that transforms the world one person at a time.

Good Friday

My God, my God, why have you forsaken me?
–Matt 27:46

THESE ARE THE WORDS that both Matthew and Mark remember as Christ's final words. They are very troubling words. Luke recalls Christ's final words differently, "Father, into your hands I commit my spirit." John, likewise, recalls them differently, "It is finished." These are much less troublesome.

Nothing is more memorable than dying words and the reporting of the crucifixion in the gospels has all the markings of historical reporting. While we don't know for certain, it seems that only John and the women in Jesus's life were at the cross. So, it is tempting to assume that John's version, "It is finished" is most reliable and that the versions of the others rely on hearsay, but the hearsay is from the women at the foot of the cross, and, therefore, must be taken seriously. Since we believe the gospels to be inspired, we must assume that God intended to reveal something of himself by these accounts. How can that help us understand the desperation of that final moment?

"...why have you forsaken me?" These are words of desolation and betrayal, words of profound darkness, words of despair, words of unbearable spiritual pain, pain worse than death itself, pain from which death is actually a relief. These are the same words we utter when we ask where was God at the holocaust, where is God when a beloved child, parent, or spouse is lost to tragedy, where is God to the hopelessly isolated and depressed?

These are the words we use when we hold God responsible for the events of life. Often, we make the excuse for God that his wisdom is beyond our understanding, that an event only appears bad because we do not fully know God's plan. But, when really tough things happen, we easily wonder what kind of God either causes or allows such evil. What kind of God allows the torture of the innocent? What kind of God destroys his only son? It is easy to become angry with God or think either that we have been forsaken by God or that there is no God.

Could such feelings be the final experience of Christ's death? Is it so unthinkable? Can it be that our torment at the contemplation of evil is but a pale reflection of God's own torment? Is God's pain an impossible contradiction? Or is it the ultimate assurance of His love?

Could it be that Christ took on our sins, our humanity, our human failings, our pain to this extent? Was this the ultimate compassion, this participation in our despair, in our isolation? Was Christ showing us that however dark and desolate our soul, however isolated, however lonely, however painful, even however hopeless, it is still possible nevertheless to have the faith and love to say, "My God, my God..."?

Can it be that the truest expression of God is compassion and that he rejoices when we rejoice, that he grieves when we grieve, that he experiences our joy and our pain? Can it be that we are most like him when we share one another's joy and pain? Can it be that Christ was showing us just how far we should be willing to go in loving one another? Was he showing us that love is not just a convenient exercise in civility, but a participation in one another's joy and pain, and, so, one another's needs? Was this the final example of "love one another as I have loved you?" Does this moment set the standard for Christian love far beyond our customary sanitized, remote, detached, safe, comfortable, convenient, and self-affirming disengagement?

"My God, my God!" That is a powerful affirmation. How can the despair of "why have you forsaken me" and the faith of "my God, my God" coexist? This moment of profound physical, emotional, and spiritual pain was recalled by Matthew and Mark as a moment of affirmation. Can it be that in the knowledge that God shares our pain, or, better, that we participate in God's pain, we too can affirm with faith and love, "my God, my God"?

Postscript

3/15/2001

I wish I could find the words now to express how powerful an affirmation this is as I cry, "My God, my God, why have you forsaken me?" I understand more fully what Jesus meant.

Faith

Faith is the nexus of our kinship to God, an epiphany of being that emerges from immersion in grace.

FAITH IS A DIFFICULT NOTION. Faith is the capacity to see a reality beyond what our senses and our reasoning reveal to us. It runs counter to our nature and to our culture. It is difficult for us to believe with our whole being in a personal and loving God. From years of Catholic and Jesuit upbringing I have known that one is supposed to have a personal relationship with the Lord and that the Father in heaven loves us. How does one have a personal relationship with someone who died 2000 years ago. How does one believe in a Father in heaven, wherever that is. Is Faith a mere cerebral assent to what formal religion teaches us? What makes our belief in God different from a belief in astrology? Neither has a basis in our senses or rational reasoning. But one is superstition and the other is Faith. Faith is a gift, one that we tend to not accept graciously, if at all. Faith changes us in ways we would rather not change. Faith seeps into our life slowly, and sometimes we lose it. Sometimes, we let our guard down and Faith rushes in, we are touched, Faith is no longer just an intellectual nod, but becomes a powerful insight, uncluttered by the usual trivialities of our routine life.

The Hebrew and biblical context of "faith" and "belief" is trust or reliance ("I have faith in you" or "I believe in you"). Biblically, Faith is trust or confidence in God and reliance on His Providence. Abraham had faith in God's promise to make him a great nation despite all evidence to the contrary (Gen 15). The Psalmist rejoices in God's Providence (Pss 31:1-11). Paul echoes, "Now faith is being sure of what we hope for and certain of what we do not see (Heb 11:1)." Trustworthiness of outcome is evident in Matt 9:22: "your faith has healed you." and Mark 9:23: "Everything is possible for him who believes." Faith is paramount to Jesus, Matt 8:10: "I tell you the truth, I have not found anyone in Israel with such great faith." Matt 9:22: "Take heart, daughter, your faith has healed you."

Sadly, the etymology of current meanings for these words brings us "faith" as "creed," a system of beliefs, principles, dogmas, and opinions. "Belief" shifts from reliance on God's Providence to mental acceptance of something as true. Epistemology absconds with faith and reason as underpinnings of knowledge. Faith is too precious a gift to be reduced to an epistemological adjunct to reason. Too often we take the question, "Do you believe in God?" to be "Do you believe in the existence of God?" These are two vastly different questions. The first relates to faith, the latter to knowledge. It is not uncommon for religious thinking to confound these two, because, as a habit, we use the word "believe" without any distinction between its two very different meanings of "I think this to be so" and "I rely on you." We entrench ourselves in a quagmire of misconception when we speak of "faith" and the "content of faith" as though "faith" was the act of assent and the "content of faith" was what was given assent to. Since the "content of faith" is equated to scriptural revelation and magisterial doctrine, this reduces faith to a willful act of assenting to doctrine. Assent to doctrine is not what impressed Jesus nor was it the focus of the early church:

> **Matt 9:29:** "According to your faith will it be done to you."
>
> **Acts 20:21:** "I have declared to both Jews and Greeks that they must ... have faith in our Lord Jesus."
>
> **1 Tim 3:13:** "Those who have served well gain...great assurance in their faith in Christ Jesus."

John 20:31: "...by believing you may have life in his name."

This faith that so impressed Jesus and which was so important to the early church is integrally fused to God Himself and is not mere creed about the idea of God.

Faith is the answer to "whether" or "who," not "what." Faith is not a matter of doctrine. Faith is not mere consent to a Creed. It is personal knowing of God Himself. Faith is a handshake with God. Faith is a miracle of profound perception and awareness of God that transforms contraries. Faith is possible only if we are willing to look God in the face (John 3:15) "that everyone who believes in Him may have eternal life." With Faith, we draw in God's own breath. We cannot turn our back on God and still have Faith. Mark 16:16: "Whoever believes and is baptized will be saved, but whoever does not believe will be condemned." "Believe" means to know God Himself (the Song of Solomon), not merely to know about God (cognition); it does not mean anything so trifling as "to have an opinion" or "to think." Faith means to believe in someone, that is, to trust, rather than to believe in something, that is, to abide in ideology. Faith is personal and requires relationship. "Yes, I believe God exists." is not the answer of Faith, but, rather, "Yes, I rely on God."

Just as Christ was engendered in Mary through the Holy Spirit upon her "fiat," so also Faith is born in us through God's grace upon our willingness to receive the Holy Spirit. Faith is both a gift of God's grace and our choice to receive it. Faith is the nexus of our kinship to God, an epiphany of being that emerges from immersion in grace. It is expansive and creative and fills our whole being. It cannot be diminished except by our own choice not to heed its draw.

If we believe truly then we do God's work, we love God and we love our neighbor. Matt 25:40: "I tell you the truth, whatever you did for one of the least of these brothers of mine, you did for me." Faith is awareness of other; hope is expectation of other; love is union with other. If we merely give consent to doctrine without carrying out God's work, which is to care for His children, then "...faith by itself... not accompanied by action, is dead" –Jas 2:17. Doctrine, alone, is limiting and sterile. Assent to truth is not the experience of truth.

Faith is knowledge of God Himself, and thus unconditional reliance and confidence in the trustworthiness of a loving Father and His Providence.

Salvation comes from Faith that transforms the world

> **Matt 25:34 -36:** Come, you who are blessed by my Father; take your inheritance, the kingdom prepared for you since the creation of the world. For I was hungry and you gave me something to eat, I was thirsty and you gave me something to drink, I was a stranger and you invited me in, I needed clothes and you clothed me, I was sick and you looked after me, I was in prison and you came to visit me.

Salvation is not conditioned by articles of Creed, by subscription to theological propositions or doctrines, even those considered by Christianity to be fundamental. Salvation is not dependent on what we think of Trinity, Sacrament, Original Sin, Scripture or Tradition, Virgin Birth, or Papacy. Examined doctrine and the consistency of doctrine, the intellectual recognition of theological truth can be nourishing, and should be sought as good, but, alone, they neither produce nor sustain Faith, nor assure Salvation. At judgment, we will not be queried about doctrine or how we exercised religious rituals, but we will be judged on what we did about "the least," Christ Himself, unequivocally, the reality of Eucharist. We ignore Matt 25:31-46 at our own peril.

> **Matt 25:31-46:** When the Son of Man comes in his glory, and all the angels with him, he will sit on his glorious throne. All the nations will be gathered before him, and he will separate the people one from another as a shepherd separates the sheep from the goats. He will put the sheep on his right and the goats on his left. Then the King will say to those on his right, 'Come, you who are blessed by my Father; take your inheritance, the kingdom prepared for you since the creation of the world. For I was hungry and you gave me something to eat, I was thirsty and you gave me something to drink, I was a stranger and you invited me in, I needed clothes and you clothed me, I was sick and you looked after me, I was in prison and you came to visit me.' Then the righteous will answer him,

'Lord, when did we see you hungry and feed you, or thirsty and give you something to drink? When did we see you a stranger and invite you in, or needing clothes and clothe you? When did we see you sick or in prison and go to visit you?' The King will reply, 'Truly I tell you, whatever you did for one of the least of these brothers and sisters of mine, you did for me.' Then he will say to those on his left, 'Depart from me, you who are cursed, into the eternal fire prepared for the devil and his angels. For I was hungry and you gave me nothing to eat, I was thirsty and you gave me nothing to drink, I was a stranger and you did not invite me in, I needed clothes and you did not clothe me, I was sick and in prison and you did not look after me.' They also will answer, 'Lord, when did we see you hungry or thirsty or a stranger or needing clothes or sick or in prison, and did not help you?' He will reply, 'Truly I tell you, whatever you did not do for one of the least of these, you did not do for me.' Then they will go away to eternal punishment, but the righteous to eternal life.

Faith vs. Works

THE QUESTION OF WHETHER salvation comes through faith or good works (which precipitated the first schism) was fundamentally stupid. Clearly, salvation comes from both. Faith without good works is empty and not real, Matt 25:45: "whatever you did not do for one of the least of these, you did not do for me." The Scriptures are explicit on the issue, and it is amazing that it was ever a point of contention.

> **Jas 2:14-26:** What good is it, my brothers, if a man claims to have faith but has no deeds? Can such faith save him? Suppose a brother or sister is without clothes and daily food. If one of you says to him, 'Go, I wish you well; keep warm and well fed,' but does nothing about his physical needs, what good is it? In the same way, faith by itself, if it is not accompanied by action, is dead. But someone will say, 'You have faith; I have deeds.' Show me your faith without deeds, and I will show you my faith by what I do. You believe that there is one God. Good! Even the demons believe that–and shudder. You foolish man, do you want evidence that faith without deeds is useless? Was not our ancestor Abraham considered righteous for what he did when he offered his son Isaac on the altar? You see that his faith and his actions were working together, and his faith was made complete by what he did. And the scripture was fulfilled that says,

> 'Abraham believed God, and it was credited to him as righteousness,' and he was called God's friend. You see that a person is justified by what he does and not by faith alone. In the same way, was not even Rahab the prostitute considered righteous for what she did when she gave lodging to the spies and sent them off in a different direction? As the body without the spirit is dead, so faith without deeds is dead.

I wonder how much this unambiguous scriptural text had to do with Luther's distaste for James.

The Church's doctrine on indulgences and its practice of effectively selling indulgences did not help the matter. Despite efforts to do so, I do not understand or subscribe to the Church's notions of indulgences and temporal punishment for sin. These doctrines operate on the assumption of divine retribution, contradicted by Job and Christ's own words. It also supposes that the dead remain in time instead of entering eternity. How can there be temporal punishment in eternity? The same limitations apply to the doctrine of purgatory. It makes as little sense to me today as it likely did for Luther in his day. I am not prepared, however, to separate myself from Christ's own Church over it. I do not believe the doctrine to be even remotely connected to true faith and suspect it is a bureaucratic remnant that most of the Church would like to pretend never existed. Unfortunately, some things that do not matter are hard to let go.

Creation

TIME PROCEEDS FROM past to future. The past can be sized and located in any manner we wish, from microseconds to eons. So, too, the future. But the present cannot, for the present is an undefinable moment sandwiched between the past and the future. The window of the past can move anywhere on the time-line up to the present. So, too, the future from the opposite direction. The present is the barrier between the past and the future. But, as soon as I begin to demarcate the present, it is already in the past. If I anticipate the present, however closely, it is still in the future. The present moment cannot be digitized or otherwise quantified. The present cannot be seized. For good reason, the expression is "*carpe diem*," not "*carpe temporem*." The present is as undefinable as eternity. The present can only be identified as between past and future and eternity as outside time altogether. Can it be that the present is intersection with eternity? The eternal now? Eternity is not just a very long time. Eternity is not always; it is not forever; it is not "for all times;" it is not "from the beginning;" it is not "to the end of time." Eternity is outside time and is inseparable from God. The ontological necessity for eternity outside time and creation outside the Big Bang are the profound realities of existence.

To create is to draw being from non-being. There is nothing outside creation except God. God is transcendent. He is outside his creation. His creation is not Himself and, while it is a faithful reflection, it remains a reflection. A reflection, however faithful, can never be what it reflects. This is the oversight of pantheism. The existence of matter without creation is contradiction. Stubborn refusal to recognize this metaphysical necessity for creation is the failure of materialism. God is neither temporal nor spatial. Failure to recognize this, either by habit of perception or refusal to accept the possibility of being outside the limits of space/time inevitably leads the thinking person to reject God.

> **Heb 11:3:** By faith we understand that the universe was formed at God's command, so that what is seen was not made out of what was visible.

Actually, I think Paul overstates the case. Faith is not required to understand the point. Human reason suffices. God is a metaphysical necessity for the existence (creation) of the space/time universe. For man, creation was not an event in history but is a continuing process in time. God created the universe and all in it in becoming, an unfolding, a progressively sharper reflection of the creator, a continuing creation, not a static creation. Evolution is creation in time, a process of being and growth. Until the unfolding of consciousness, the creation of man through the process of evolution, all creation was in harmony with its creator, that is, the process was inevitable according to its very nature. The innate force within all creation to move towards perfection by trying all possibilities became, in the attainment of consciousness, centered on itself, condemned by its narrow vision, to struggle with moral evil, genetic to man's nature, moral evil having become a possibility realized. Nothing can compel creation to continue unless consciousness itself, man, wills it to continue by turning from itself to another. This was original sin. The sin of Adam was that of Narcissus. It was that of the fallen angels. Redemption, the undoing of Adam's sin, through God-centered consciousness, became possible through a new creation in the personal intervention of God himself in his creation in the person of Christ.

Why do so many Christians view evolution as demonic? Why this insistence on the literal reading of Genesis creation? Do they not see that the authors of Genesis took a timely myth and turned it into God's message that God created the universe and made it good, that all his creatures are a growing reflection of Himself? Do they not see that to be the message of Genesis and not the step-by-step particulars? Do they not see the wonder of God's reflection becoming increasingly realized? Or are they confused by literalness to see creation as a metaphysical instantaneous reality? Do they equate the notion of "myth" with that of "untrue?" Do they reduce evolution to mere transformism? Do they confuse evolution with the arrogant naivete of some of its materialistic proponents? It is unfortunate that materialists see evolution as the intellectual justification for their negation of purpose, design, and intelligence in the universe and, thus, their negation of God.

Evolution answers the question of "how" our world came to be as it is today, but it does not address the "why." Genesis addresses the "why," and, for those who understand, not the "how." The "how" in Genesis is purely incidental metaphor, a story on which to attach the "why" for man's existence. Therefore, fatuous attempts to create contorted concordance between the "how" of Genesis and intellectually valid scientific descriptions of the origins of the world and mankind are all useless exercises in silliness. It matters little if the attempt is to explain how light and vegetation came to be before the sun or how relativistic theory can account for a six-day creation. It is all shameful foolishness arising from a failure to recognize the essential message in the myth. Sadly, fundamentalists who insist on the literal meaning of the Genesis story miss the whole point. Equally sad, materialists who stipulate that "why" is a stupid question miss the obvious. I doubt that they would question the self-evident redundancy of the principle of ontological non-contradiction. I wonder why they do not likewise perceive the ontological necessity for creation: regardless of how matter came to be organized with apparent design, matter at one point still had to come into being from non-being, and that, by definition, ontological necessity, is creation. This is not just an admission that we do not understand where matter came from or that we do not understand how non-being can become being: it is true, we do not comprehend, but, more, we are compelled by definition, not ignorance, to recognize it as creation. If we can stipulate the ontological necessity for creation, then we can admit of the possibility of intelligence and, thus, of validity for the question "why" or even "who." Materialists despairingly dispense with this as metaphysics. And so it is, but why do they consider the rigors of logic applied to being itself less credible than the same principles applied to physical evidence? It is a peculiar bias that cannot be overcome, because it is a contradiction to obtain or present physical evidence for being before being.

Creation can only be attributed to God. It can be attributed to man only in a metaphorical sense, that is, by viewing man as an analogy for God, which is a useful device for conceptualizing God. Man's metaphor for creation is his own truly creative works where he brings existence where none was before. Poetry and music are accurate metaphors for creation. In these, elements of mind and spirit come together to grow, develop, and explode into transcendent power that is beyond their mere compilation. Like God's own creation, poetry and music acquire a life and will of it own, but, nevertheless, like Creation, remains a reflection of the creator, and, although free to act according to it's own nature, it still bears the imprint and influence of its creator.

Evil

IF GOD WERE BOTH GOOD and omnipotent he would have created only good, a perfect creation without pain or evil. But we all know that creation is both imperfect and abundant in pain and evil. This is the ageless problem of pain. Could God have created a perfect world without evil? I think not. It is tempting to think that God's inability to do so imposes a limit on his omnipotence. As CS Lewis would remind us, God cannot create a contradiction because doing so would contradict God Himself. Although Matthew tells us Matt 19:26: "with God all things are possible," this does not mean that God is capable of intrinsic nonsense. Christ Himself recognized this: Matt 26:42: "My Father, *if it is not possible* for this cup to be taken away unless I drink it, may your will be done." Creation without evil is as much a self-contradiction as a coin with only one side. The prophet Isaiah realized this, Isa 45:7: "I form the light and create darkness, I bring prosperity and create disaster; I, the LORD, do all these things." And as Job teaches us, evil happens without deference to fairness or convenience and is not a consequence of sin. This was affirmed by Christ:

> **John 9:1-3:** As he went along, he saw a man blind from birth. His disciples asked him, 'Rabbi, who sinned, this man or his parents, that he was born blind?' 'Neither this man nor his parents sinned,' said Jesus, 'but this happened so that the work of God might be displayed in his life.' And the man was made to see.

The Genesis account of creation and the Fall is unambiguously allegory. This does not mean it is not true, just that it requires interpretation. It is the earliest Judaic look at the problem of pain. The Fall is troublesome. It is clear from biological evolution that Adam had to be a crowd, so the traditional explanations are unsatisfying. Genesis tells us that God created all of creation good and that it was spoiled by man's sin of disobedience.

Just as Genesis exploited the contemporary myths, were it being written today, I have no doubt the authors would use evolution as the underlying myth, because evolution meshes very well with the Genesis message of creation by a loving God. Regardless, the Genesis creation account was clearly not written to inform us about paleontology. It was written to assure us that God created the temporal universe and made it good, imprinting it with Himself. He set it on an inevitable course of development (the Big Bang) that reflects Him and His goodness, growing towards an ever-clearer reflection of Himself. Creation tries all possibilities imprinted in it from the beginning and progresses through time (evolution) closer to its Creator. Those who object to this from entropy misunderstand entropy, fail to recognize the obvious progressive nature of evolution from the evidence itself, and overlook the spiritual dimension. The rise of consciousness resulted in the ability to choose, free will, and with it came moral evil. Until consciousness, evolution moved creation in harmony with God's own imprint, but after consciousness (man), creation acquired the ability to move according to its own choices. Harmony with God's imprint was no longer inevitable. Consciousness centered creation on man rather than God. This was the Fall. It spoiled not only consciousness itself, but the evolutionary creative process as well. The undoing of the Fall can only come from a centering of consciousness back to God.

Suffering poses a problem for us. Suffering of the innocent tells us clearly that our inclination to think that God controls the universe on the principle of reward and retribution is misguided. Why did not God stop the holocaust? Why does he not stop the death of hundreds in a plane crash or the death of thousands in an earthquake? Why does he not stop bullets in war or senseless killings? How can an all-loving and omnipotent God stand by and watch the slaughter of innocents? If we say that God is looking at the greater good, then do the ends justify the means for God? If we say that we are too limited to understand God's plan, then we say that the slaughter of innocents is part of his plan. How can an all-loving God include the slaughter of innocents in his plan? Can it be that God is not omnipotent after all? If God is the master of all creation and all proceeds according to his will or plan, does that mean that God micro-manages the universe? Has not God set the universe in motion on a path towards perfection that is a reflection of Himself? Physical and moral evil happens. Physical evil is an inevitable consequence of process. Moral evil, while not inevitable, is a predictable consequence of consciousness. God does not interfere with the march of creation. Physical evil is mindless, moral evil is mindful. Physical evil arises from the march of creation stumbling over itself; moral evil arises from consciousness obsessed with itself. But even physical evil is impossible without consciousness to recognize it.

Why is God most visible, most palpable, in the presence of suffering? Why does God become increasingly invisible with increasing comfort? Why is pain redemptive? What is sin? Why was dying on the cross necessary for the Father's will? How does pain redeem? Can it be that consciousness focused on itself can never attain or find what it seeks? Can it be that pain, arising from awareness of separation, draws the attention of consciousness away from itself? It is in our very nature to turn away from pain. We can do so by undoing the pain, recognizing our humanity and our separation from God, and that is salutary, or we can anesthetize ourselves to it, and it will overcome us. The more consciousness focuses outside itself the more it loves. Consciousness cannot remain focused on another (love) unless it expects (hope) to unite with the other, and it can do neither if it does not have awareness of the other (faith). It cannot be aware of the other unless its attention is drawn away from itself. As our awareness of the other increases, we experience to the point of tears our own emptiness and long to fill the emptiness with the other. Even a slight filling of that emptiness brings joy and tears of joy. We weep for the difference between what could be and what is. When we weep, our tears are a pale reflection of God's tears. Tears testify to what we see by Faith, that in justice, decency, and compassionate acts we see a loving God. When we weep at the sight of evil and goodness in the lives of ordinary or extraordinary people, we do so because by Faith we are reminded that the Word of God is incarnate among us. There is nothing in human experience, the human condition, other than pain that can draw man's awareness inexorably outside himself.

Truth

TRUTH IS TRUTH. That should be self-evident to any thinking person. However, it is very easy for us overlook certitude of truth in today's pluralistic world. Democracies, in particular, engender a mind-set where every opinion, every view, every idea is presumed to be equal in value as any other. This is the new relativism. There is no objective absolute truth. Tolerance for all except intolerance (or what is interpreted as intolerance) is the only acceptable paradigm. This translates into the general philosophy that there is, in fact, only one absolute truth: the truth that there is no absolute truth!

It is fashionable to view the notion of objective truth as limiting to enlightenment. The ontological contradiction of this position escapes too many of us. Fuzzy logic is supreme. Critical thinking is too burdensome. As C.S. Lewis was fond of reminding us, there is only one correct answer to a sum, all other answers are wrong, although some are closer to the correct answer than others. Truth, as Lewis clearly saw, is both objective and unique. This uniqueness is so uncomfortable to some that they make the intellectually cowardly profession of "different kinds of truth." Physical, material, and mathematical certitude is one thing, but philosophical, ethical, spiritual, theological certitudes are a different matter. The degree of difficulty to perceive truth is taken as a measure of relativity. If I do not have the mental capability to sum numbers, does that mean that the sum is relative? Is there a difference if I come up with a disparate sum because I cannot add or commit an immoral act because I have a defective conscience? Does it make sense to excuse me by saying that my sum and my moral view was right for me? If I am color blind and see a red object as green, does my insistence that it is green make it green? The underlying presumption today seems to be the universalization of the marketing precept that perception is reality. If something is perceived as correct then it surely must be correct, and, since perceptions are so diverse, then surely reality is diverse. There can be no absolute reality, no absolute truth, no absolute right, no absolute wrong. The new relativism has turned reality into a straw man.

This contemporary relativism is insidious and dangerous. It robs science and art of objective value. Homeopathy is as relevant as genuine medicine. Astrology becomes a valid science. Every ambiguous polished double-speak becomes a patent unquestioned truism. Every inane created object becomes true art in the declaration. Every abnormality becomes an alternate normality. Anyone who dares question the liberation of this relativism is obviously marred by antiquated preconception. Of course, since there is no objective truth, then revelation can have no meaning. "The truth shall set you free" loses all meaning. Clearly, the absence of truth sets you free. If there were an objective truth, it would be confining, not liberating: the new relativism is dangerously seductive.

Two sources of truth, both from God, reason and revelation, therefore, cannot be in conflict. Scripture and tradition are vehicles of revelation. That is truth!

Body-Soul

So will it be with the resurrection of the dead. The body that is sown is perishable, it is raised imperishable; it is sown in dishonor, it is raised in glory; it is sown in weakness, it is raised in power; it is sown a natural body, it is raised a spiritual body.
–1 Cor 15:42-44

DUALISM OF BODY AND SOUL is a confounding Hellenic influence on Christianity, an inclination to see the human person as a composite of a distinct mortal material body and an immortal spiritual soul. This dichotomy is artificial.

The human person is an integral unit, a single nature. The biology of man imposes the creation, growth, and epiphany of soul as a dimension of man. The soul of man is inherent in the nature of man and does not demand a special infusion of soul by divine intervention. The soul is the identity of man and transcends his material existence. Human life reflects growth, formation, and transformation of the soul as the person experiences and makes choices that form and define it. Because of this, it is a sin against man, and thus against God, to deprive any person of this good by depriving any human person of life or freedom. Likewise, man sins against his own nature and God when he deprives his soul of its integrity. Sins against integrity deprive the soul of growth and lead to emptiness and isolation.

Just as life escapes the confines of inanimate matter and consciousness escapes those of biology, so too the soul escapes the confines of mortal existence. Does this mean that on death of the body, the soul rises out of the body and goes to heaven or hell? That is a common naive simplification that is a consequence of dualism and spatial/temporal perspective. It also naively supposes that heaven or hell are places. That would limit heaven or hell to space/time. Heaven and hell make no sense unless they are outside space/time. They must be in eternity, and they must be states of existence. Heaven, by definition, must be unity with God, eternal love. Hell, separation from God, eternal isolation. For God to exist in the confines of space/time is a contradiction. Man escapes his own mortality when he passes from a spatial/temporal universe into eternity. Eternity is outside time. Questions about life after death arising from a temporal perspective are meaningless. We go to God by passing into eternity and eternity is neither a place nor a time. For one passing into eternity, considerations of space or time are without meaning. In eternity, we are not absorbed into God as a mere drop absorbed into the ocean: a loving God, by definition, must esteem our integrity and, thus, must preserve our personal individuality.

Mystical Body

Because there is one loaf, we, who are many, are one body, for we all partake of the one loaf.
–1Cor 10:17

A DISTINGUISHING CHARACTERISTIC of the Catholic Church is its preservation of the Pauline doctrine of the Mystical Body of Christ or the Communion of Saints. The Church is the assembly of all the saints, living and dead, into the one Body of Christ with Christ as its head. All the members are connected to one another through and for Christ. This truth was frequently identified by Christ Himself and was championed emphatically by Paul. Analogous beliefs are held by many non-Christian peoples such as Africans and native American Indians. The concept is recognized by many non-Catholic Christian faiths, but it has been stripped of much of its mystical reality. Much as the real presence of Christ in the Eucharist has been diluted, so too the reality of the Mystical Body of Christ has been diluted to a point where it is not so incredible.

> **1 Cor 12:12-27:** The body is a unit, though it is made up of many parts; and though all its parts are many, they form one body. So it is with Christ. For we were all baptized by one Spirit into one body–whether Jews or Greeks, slave or free–and we were all given the one Spirit to drink. Now the body is not made up of one part but of many. If the foot should say,

'Because I am not a hand, I do not belong to the body,' it would not for that reason cease to be part of the body. And if the ear should say, 'Because I am not an eye, I do not belong to the body,' it would not for that reason cease to be part of the body. If the whole body were an eye, where would the sense of hearing be? If the whole body were an ear, where would the sense of smell be? But in fact, God has arranged the parts in the body, every one of them, just as he wanted them to be. If they were all one part, where would the body be? As it is, there are many parts, but one body. The eye cannot say to the hand, 'I don't need you!' And the head cannot say to the feet, 'I don't need you!' On the contrary, those parts of the body that seem to be weaker are indispensable, and the parts that we think are less honorable we treat with special honor. And the parts that are unpresentable are treated with special modesty, while our presentable parts need no special treatment. But God has combined the members of the body and has given greater honor to the parts that lacked it, so that there should be no division in the body, but that its parts should have equal concern for each other. If one part suffers, every part suffers with it; if one part is honored, every part rejoices with it. Now you are the body of Christ, and each one of you is a part of it.

Rom 12:4-8: Just as each of us has one body with many members, and these members do not all have the same function, so in Christ we who are many form one body, and each member belongs to all the others. We have different gifts, according to the grace given us. If a man's gift is prophesying, let him use it in proportion to his faith. If it is serving, let him serve; if it is teaching, let him teach; if it is encouraging, let him encourage; if it is contributing to the needs of others, let him give generously; if it is leadership, let him govern diligently; if it is showing mercy, let him do it cheerfully.

PART 2

FUNDAMENTALS OF FAITH

Bible

SCRIPTURE, THE BIBLE, is a collection of God's love letters to man. It is hardly possible to read scripture with an open heart and not be deeply moved.

While the Bible is the word of God, it is not the transcribed word of God in which the human contribution has been thoroughly subjugated or suppressed. There is no mistaking Jeremiah for Ezekiel. Luke is unmistakably not Matthew. The differences do not reflect differences or nuances in God's message, but differences in the human authors. If there is one message clear from all of Scripture it is that God loves us as we are and that he respects our free will. To suggest that God would subvert the human authors of Scripture contradicts the very intent of Scripture itself. Scripture attests to its human component:

> **Luke 1:3:** "Therefore, since I myself have carefully investigated everything from the beginning."
>
> **2 Mac 15:38:** "If it is well told and to the point, that is what I myself desired; if it is poorly done and mediocre, that was the best I could do."

And, too, it attests to its divine contribution:

> **Acts 4:25:** "You spoke by the Holy Spirit through the mouth of your servant"
>
> 2 **Pet 3:15:** "... just as our dear brother Paul also wrote you with the wisdom that God gave him."
>
> **2 Pet 1:21:** "... men spoke from God as they were carried along by the Holy Spirit."

Through the Holy Spirit, human writers were inspired (from the Latin '*inspirare*', meaning to breath in) to transmit God's message. While the human writer used his own wits, talents, and skills to write, the message was God's, and, so, in a true sense, God was the author. This does not mean, however, that God dictated His message, that the human writer was a mere recorder. The message was God's, but the literature was man's. It is essential, then to understand and master the human literature to fully perceive God's message. This is both an art and a science. This exegesis must use all scholarly methods possible for understanding the literature in its own context. This is particularly important when considering books of the Bible that use literary forms that are alien to our own culture and thus more likely to be misunderstood.

While Christ Himself did not personally write scripture, He did use some literary tools to present His teachings. Parables were second nature to Christ. The parable is an excellent example of a literary tool used to convey profound truth by using a fictional story. It is important to recognize that Jesus Himself used storytelling to convey truth and that the story itself could easily be fiction without in anyway compromising the truth conveyed.

It is important to recognize that literary fiction does not mean that the meaning is false. On the contrary, it is commonplace in the literature of all human cultures to use fiction to convey the greatest truths. This is the place of myth. Unfortunately, for many, the word "myth" is the emotional equivalent of "not true." Closing of mind in this way is very damaging to understanding. The Bible is a collection of diverse literatures, ranging from myth, to poetry, to history, to parables, to instruction, to narratives, to letters, to some uniquely biblical hybrids. To hear God's message, to hear His Word, that is, to correctly understand what we read or hear, it is essential to first understand the word in context. Then, with the guidance of the Holy Spirit, we come to hear God's own message in the written word. Yes, the Bible is God's word, and it is without error. To conclude from this, however, that every word of the Bible means literally what it says, without interpretation, is as foolish as to think that when one says it is raining "cats and dogs" cats and dogs are in fact falling out of the sky.

Christ Himself recognized the Jewish Books of the Old Testament as the word of God. The early Christian Church, likewise, recognized this and added what we consider today as the New Testament. There are some who insist that Holy Scripture itself is the unique source of God's word and authority. There is a self-evident internal inconsistency in this. Nowhere in Scripture, that is, nowhere in any inspired book of the Bible, is there any stipulation as to what writings are considered or recognized as "biblical." So, the Bible's very constitution relies on authority outside itself to identify or stipulate exactly what writings make up the Bible. For the original Jewish scripture, we must turn to Jewish authority. For the Christian Bible, we must rely on Church authority to define the "Canon" of scripture. There may be some minor disputes about exactly which books are included (the apocrypha), but, regardless, the Bible's "Canon" relies on authority outside the Bible itself.

This does not diminish the Bible in any way: it remains God's loving word to His children. But, does it make sense that a loving Father would write these letters to His children and then be quiet? On the contrary, our loving Father continues to speak, guide, and stand by us with His Church, our brothers and sisters, the saints, the family of God, and even by continuing to inspire through influences around us today, secular as well as sacred. So, while the Bible is a treasured and very special collection of messages from a loving Father, the Bible is not an archived recording from a now silent God. God is not dead, nor is He quiet.

Eucharist

THE EUCHARIST IS A distinguishing character of the Catholic Church in that the bread and wine of the last supper and its reenactment according to Christ's own instructions in the liturgy of the Mass is believed to be exactly what Christ said that it was, His body and blood. Christ is believed to be truly present in the bread and wine of the Eucharist. As it should be, the celebration of the Eucharist is the pivotal focus of Faith in the Catholic Church.

The scripture is taken at its word. I find it odd that those of the Fundamentalist persuasion do not. Some Churches do not go as far as to speak of the "Real Presence," as do Catholics, but speak instead of the "sacramental presence." It seems to me that this is the same as speaking of the "Real Presence" since a sacrament is a symbol that truly effects what it symbolizes.

The Eucharist is the most perspicuous of the sacraments:

> **John 6:53-58:** Jesus said to them, 'I tell you the truth, unless you eat the flesh of the Son of Man and drink his blood, you have no life in you. Whoever eats my flesh and drinks my blood has eternal life, and I will

> raise him up at the last day. For my flesh is real food and my blood is real drink. Whoever eats my flesh and drinks my blood remains in me, and I in him. Just as the living Father sent me and I live because of the Father, so the one who feeds on me will live because of me. This is the bread that came down from heaven. Your forefathers ate manna and died, but he who feeds on this bread will live forever.'

Most clearly, the Eucharist unites us with Christ and thus separates us from sin, Matt 26:28: "This is my blood of the covenant, which is poured out for many for the forgiveness of sins." The Eucharist unites us with each other in the Church, the communion of saints:

> **1 Cor 10:16 -17:** "Is not the cup of thanksgiving for which we give thanks a participation in the blood of Christ? And is not the bread that we break a participation in the body of Christ? Because there is one loaf, we, who are many, are one body, for we all partake of the one loaf." Since we are all one in the Eucharist, we are called to see Christ in each other and be Christ to each other, most particularly those in greatest need of Providence,"
>
> **Matt 25:40:** "I tell you the truth, whatever you did for one of the least of these brothers of mine, you did for me."

Thus, Eucharist is not mere metaphor, nor is it magic: it calls us to bring about Christ's Kingdom on earth:

> **Luke 14:13:** "'...when you give a banquet, invite the poor, the crippled, the lame, the blind,' as Christ has done at His Eucharistic banquet."
>
> **1 John 4:16-21** "...Whoever lives in love lives in God, and God in him...We love because he first loved us.... And he has given us this command: Whoever loves God must also love his brother."

I have difficulty with the relatively recent Catholic tradition of separating the Eucharist, the consecrated bread and wine, apart from the liturgy of the last supper or the Mass and then venerate it in a Monstrance or keep vigil over the Eucharist. This is referred to as adoration of the Blessed Sacrament. Clearly, adoration has been a positive spiritual experience for many. Without being purposefully negative, this practice seems in need of perspective. Christ Himself said that the bread and wine of the Eucharist is His body and blood, and that we should eat and drink of it. He said nothing about adoration in a gold tabernacle or being displayed in a regal gold Monstrance. I fear that the practice disconnects the Blessed Sacrament from the liturgy of the Eucharist and introduces conceptual distortions that may ultimately diminish Faith rather than enhance it. Christ in the Eucharist unites us with Him and His Church, John 6:56: "He who eats my flesh and drinks my blood abides in me, and I in him."

Outside Eucharist, the Blessed Sacrament runs the risk of becoming a superstition of homunculus. There is an intuitive inconsistency in this practice in that the historical Christ would be at best uncomfortable with its pomp and regality. Treating the bread and wine as though each crumb or drop spilled upon the floor is somehow a piece of Jesus is a reflection of the problem. Proper reverence for the Blessed Sacrament is corrupted into superstition. Retaining unused consecrated bread in a gold tabernacle and asserting that this is the appropriate abode for Christ seems to me to miss the point of both Eucharist and Christ's core mission to the poor altogether. Christ would not choose to abide in a gold tabernacle or display Himself in gold Monstrance that is reminiscent of some kind of pagan divinity. This tradition of adoration is reminiscent of Peter's impulsive response to the Transfiguration, Luke 9:33: "Master, it is good for us to be here. Let us put up three shelters – one for you, one for Moses and one for Elijah." While these practices, clearly, are designed to emphasize unambiguously the doctrine of the Real Presence, to which I absolutely subscribe, it is my perception that this tradition is so inconsistent with Christ Himself as to instill a superstitious concept rather than a sacramental one, and that, ultimately, this leads to disbelief, which may account in part for the sad statistics that claim that less than half of all Catholics believe in the Real Presence.

The philosophical explanation of transubstantiation, based on Aristotelian concepts of substance and accidents, matter and form, is so contrived as to be useless. Further, it betrays a fundamental misconception of these Aristotelian concepts. Aristotle would not recognize their use in the question of transubstantiation. Substance and accidents are metaphysical correspondents to the elemental and ionic forms of contemporary chemistry, not the "substance" of the Real Presence under the "accidents" of bread and wine. True belief in the Real Presence of Christ in the Eucharist does not require feeble philosophical explanations.

These explanations and the inconsistent traditions that separate the Eucharist from the liturgy of the Mass rob the Eucharist of its mystery and its link to the Body of Christ in the communion of saints. Not only is the bread and wine Eucharist, but we are all Eucharist in the Mystical Body, the Church. Christ also said, "...whatever you did for one of the least of these brothers of mine, you did for me." This, too, is Eucharist. Without diminishing the Real Presence of the Blessed Sacrament, I am confident from Christ's own words and personal experience that Christ is just as present in "the least" as He is in the Blessed Sacrament and one has no meaning without the other.

The Catholic custom of denying Holy Communion to Christians that do not fully recognize the truth of the Real Presence is inconsistent with Eucharist and is a sad commentary on the human shortcomings of the Church. The sacramental power of the Eucharist is not a function of consent to doctrine. The denial of Eucharist, a denial of opportunity to God's Grace, diminishes those who deny more than those who are denied

Baptism

CHRIST'S FINAL INSTRUCTION to his disciples were:

> **Matt 28:19-20:** Therefore go and make disciples of all nations, baptizing them in the name of the Father and of the Son and of the Holy Spirit, and teaching them to obey everything I have commanded you.

Christ Himself makes baptism a condition of salvation:

> **John 3:5:** I tell you the truth, no one can enter the kingdom of God unless he is born of water and the Spirit.

Baptism is "to be born of water and the Spirit,"

> **1 Pet 3:21:** this water symbolizes baptism that now saves you.... It saves you by the resurrection of Jesus Christ.

Baptism is integral to faith and salvation,

> **Mark 16:16:** Whoever believes and is baptized will be saved, but whoever does not believe will be condemned.

> **Matt 3:11:** (John) baptized you with water for repentance, ...but (Christ) baptizes you with the Holy Spirit.

Clearly, baptism has profound significance. It is an integral symbol and action of discipleship, creating a Christian identity through Faith. Baptism is the sacrament of Faith that, through the symbol of water, drowns the centricity of self that is natural to man and replaces it with the divine centricity of God's grace through the Holy Spirit.

> **Acts 2:38:** ...be baptized, every one of you, in the name of Jesus Christ for the forgiveness of your sins. And you will receive the gift of the Holy Spirit.

This is echoed by Paul:

> **Rom 6:3-4:** Don't you know that all of us who were baptized into Christ Jesus were baptized into his death? We were therefore buried with him through baptism into death in order that, just as Christ was raised from the dead through the glory of the Father, we too may live a new life.

In baptism we are truly "born again" (John 3:3) and this new life is life in Christ's Body, His Church

> **1 Cor 12:13:** For we were all baptized by one Spirit into one body--whether Jews or Greeks, slave or free–and we were all given the one Spirit to drink.

where we become Christ

> **Gal 3:27:** for all of you who were baptized into Christ have clothed yourselves with Christ.

As one body we love the whole body and tend to the needs of its members,

> **Matt 25:45-46:** He will reply, 'I tell you the truth, whatever you did not do for one of the least of these, you did not do for me.' Then they will go away to eternal punishment, but the righteous to eternal life.

This new life in the Body of Christ, His Church, is nurtured by Eucharist,

> **John 6:53:** ...unless you eat the flesh of the Son of Man and drink his blood, you have no life in you. Whoever eats my flesh and drinks my blood has eternal life.

Prayer

PRAYER IS A QUIETLY SUBMISSIVE spiritual state Luke 1:38: "I am the Lord's servant," that allows us to converse with and listen to God so as to receive the Holy Spirit, engendering God's kingdom in ourselves and the world ("fiat"), much as Mary engendered Christ, Matt 1:18: "This is how the birth of Jesus Christ came about: His mother Mary was found to be with child through the Holy Spirit." True prayer brings the realization and confirms 1 Cor 3:16: "that you yourselves are God's temple and that God's Spirit lives in you."

What is prayer? The gospels offer reliable guidelines.

> **Matt 6:6:** "But when you pray, go into your room, close the door and pray to your Father, who is unseen. And when you pray, do not keep on babbling like pagans."
>
> **Matt 6:9-13:** "This, then, is how you should pray: Our Father in heaven, hallowed be your name, your kingdom come, your will be done on earth as it is in heaven. Give us today our daily bread. Forgive us our debts, as we also have forgiven our debtors. And lead us not into temptation but deliver us from the evil one."

Christ instructs us to pray to God as OUR Father. The implications are powerful: if God is Our Father, then we, too, are Sons of God. We are all each other's brothers and sisters. We are one family. That the Father is in heaven does not mean that He is remote or far away, but, on the contrary, that He is eternal and thus permeates all of reality and thus is within our very being.

"Hallowed be your name" This is an expression of reverence, the state of mind and soul needed to converse with God.

"Your kingdom come" This is an expression of consent to the spiritual values proclaimed by Christ as opposed to the materialistic values of the world and an explicit expression of willingness to do what must be done to bring about God's kingdom, not just a wish that God do it.

"Your will be done on earth as it is in heaven." An expression of harmony with God. A confirmation of the undoing of sin and restoration of harmony by centering man on God rather than himself.

"Give us today our daily bread." This is recognition of God's providence, his promise to provide for our needs:

> **Matt 6:8:** "your Father knows what you need before you ask him."
>
> **Matt 6:28-30:** "See how the lilies of the field grow. They do not labor or spin. Yet I tell you that not even Solomon in all his splendor was dressed like one of these. If that is how God clothes the grass of the field, which is here today and tomorrow is thrown into the fire, will he not much more clothe you, O you of little faith?"

"Forgive us our debts, as we also have forgiven our debtors." This is a reminder to us of Christianity's core obligation for salvation: compassion.

> **Mark 11:25:** "And when you stand praying, if you hold anything against anyone, forgive him, so that your Father in heaven may forgive you your sins."

> **Matt 25:34:** "Come, you who are blessed by my Father, I was sick and you looked after me. Depart from me, you who are cursed, I was sick and you did not look after me."

"And lead us not into temptation but deliver us from the evil one." This is recognition of God's promise to be by our side if we but believe and trust in Him.

> **John 3:16:** "For God so loved the world that he gave his one and only Son, that whoever believes in him shall not perish but have eternal life."
>
> **Matt 28:20:** "surely I am with you always, to the very end of the age."

The Lord's prayer contains all the essential elements of true prayer: reverence, harmony, faith, love, hope. The gospel directives suggest prayer is best done in solitude: "when you pray, go into your room, close the door and pray to your Father, who is unseen." Jesus himself went into the mountains and desert and at Gethsemane, Matt 26:39: "Going a little farther, he fell with his face to the ground and prayed." The Lord's prayer, while it contains petitions, on closer examination, reveals that these very petitions are an expression of faith that is consistent with "your Father knows what you need before you ask him."

Prayer is communication between the soul and God. This is unambiguous. As in any communication, it is best done privately, without distractions. It is best done with clarity of mind and spirit. Since it is communication with God, words are not necessary, except to focus our own mind and heart. Reverence diffuses mental or spiritual restlessness that interferes with hearing God. The disciplined person accustomed to communicating with God can create the requisite solitude and ambience for prayer anywhere, be it a deserted island or a noisy public stadium. As our social nature often needs sustenance from the solidarity of common prayer, so also our sense-based nature can best be sublimated to prayer by engagement of the senses. The ambience of reverence created by the church or chapel environment is very helpful for the soul. Music that is consistent with reverence can be likewise very supportive of prayer. Music for prayer should be more than an accompaniment, background, or entertainment, all distractions at best, but prayer in itself. Gregorian chant, for example, becomes prayer on its own.

Visual support can be found in nature (a reflection of God) and even in images that we associate with holiness. Provided communication (which is listening more than it is speaking) takes place, it matters little if the form of prayer is verbalized, meditative, or contemplative, or a blend of these, or where or how it takes place. Verbal prayer is usually necessary for common prayer and is often needed even in solitude to focus the mind and will. Meditative prayer is mentally focused, while contemplative prayer is quiet listening to the voice of God. Prayer requires the fostering of a physical and mental ambience (reverence) that allows the faithful soul to lovingly sense and trustfully communicate with its creator. Prayer nurtures the soul. Prayer changes and grows the soul in harmony with God.

What of prayer of petition? Does prayer bring divine intervention? Does God pick and choose what and whose prayers to grant? Mark 11:24: "whatever you ask for in prayer, believe that you have received it, and it will be yours." That is an almost embarrassing gospel statement that is not born out by experience. Almost every misfortune, calamity, sickness, and death is testimony to its apparent foolishness. The inexorability of nature is not averted by prayer, even as it acts in defiance of suffering. Christ Himself, who certainly had the requisite faith and was an expert at prayer, prayed, "My Father, if it is possible, may this cup be taken from me. Yet not as I will, but as you will." Christ's own prayer does not meet Mark's criterion. Christ made his request conditional. How can you trust your request will be granted while at the same time setting conditions that make refusal possible? Perhaps, Mark's gospel passage on the issue is abridged ambiguously. Matthew is more complete:

> **Matt 7:7-11:** Ask and it will be given to you; seek and you will find; knock and the door will be opened to you. For everyone who asks receives; he who seeks finds; and to him who knocks, the door will be opened. Which of you, if his son asks for bread, will give him a stone? Or

> if he asks for a fish, will give him a snake? If you, then, though you are evil, know how to give good gifts to your children, how much more will your Father in heaven give good gifts to those who ask him.

Matthew's passage sounds almost as a rewording of "give us today our daily bread" and "...see how the lilies of the field grow. If that is how God clothes the grass of the field... will he not much more clothe you." Luke's version adds further insight,

> **Luke 11:13:** If you then... know how to give good gifts to your children, how much more will your Father in heaven give the Holy Spirit to those who ask him!

Luke tells us that prayer is answered with the Holy Spirit.

> **Gal 5:22-23:** But the fruit of the Spirit is love, joy, peace, patience, kindness, goodness, faithfulness, gentleness and self-control.

Surely, that is the true outcome of prayer. This is also confirmation that the petitions envisioned by the evangelists are petitions rooted in the desire to be brought into harmony with the coming of God's kingdom on earth. For that reason, it is entirely proper and consistent to pray for others, that they too may cooperate actively with the coming of God's Kingdom.

> **Rom 15:30:** "I urge you, brothers, by our Lord Jesus Christ and by the love of the Spirit, to join me in my struggle by praying to God for me."

> **Eph 6:18-20:** "And pray in the Spirit on all occasions with all kinds of prayers...be alert and always keep on praying for all the saints. Pray also for me, that whenever I open my mouth, words may be given me so that I will fearlessly make known the mystery of the gospel, for which I am an ambassador in chains. Pray that I may declare it fearlessly, as I should."

Prayer, by definition, is directed to God. We do not pray to the deceased, be they Mary or the saints, any more than we pray to the living. As we ask our friends and family to pray for us, so also, we may ask humbly the deceased, the Saints, Mary, even the Angels to pray for us. We, from Mary to the least of mankind, are all members of the same family, the communion of saints, the Pauline Body of Christ, and it is natural, that is, according to God's own design, that we care for one another and that a pivotal manifestation of that care is prayer. That is why Christ instructed us to begin with "Our Father." Christ Himself asked His friends to pray with Him in Gethsemane,

> **Matt 26:41:** Watch and pray so that you will not fall into temptation. The spirit is willing, but the body is weak.

We do not, however, pray to the saints; rather, we pray with the saints. When we ask Mary and the saints to pray for us, it is a humble recognition of the perfection of their prayer arising from their closeness to God as compared to our own imperfect prayer, arising from our separation from God. As Christ warned, "the spirit is willing, but the body is weak."

> **Rom 8:26-27:** In the same way, the Spirit helps us in our weakness. We do not know what we ought to pray for, but the Spirit himself intercedes for us with groans that words cannot express. And he who searches our hearts knows the mind of the Spirit, because the Spirit intercedes for the saints in accordance with God's will.

In prayer, the Holy Spirit draws us to God in unity with Mary and the saints. We pray with them. That is why we say, "Hail Mary, ...pray for us sinners."

We often fail to distinguish between the word "pray" or "prayer," properly directed to God, as in the Latin, "*oratio*," meaning "discourse" or "talk," and "pray" as "to entreat" or "to ask" as the Latin, "*precari*." So, we "entreat" or "ask" Mary or the saints to "pray" for us. It is unfortunate that serious misconceptions of prayer arise that lead to silly notions of medieval courtly intercessions and politics or notions of coercions and bribery of Mary, the saints, and God Himself. Prayer is an area of Christian life where discernment is critical to recognize and distinguish faith from superstition. While surely God is forgiving of individual superstitions, it is among the devil's most effective instruments to insidiously diminish faith.

The true Christian is "poor in spirit," humbly recognizing that God by His creation has provided for our needs: Matt 6:8: "your Father knows what you need before you ask him." For that reason, we often pray in thanksgiving, usually before meals, sometimes before celebrations or special events. This is entirely appropriate. But it is also a frequent Christian response to thank God whenever near misfortune is averted and thus attribute our good fortunes to His intervention. Survivors of near disasters invariably thank God for having been spared, implying or explicitly affirming divine intervention. If this is true, that God intervened, then where was He and why did He not intervene for those who are not spared? If we try to salvage this troubling issue with recourse to God's Wisdom and Will, we create a quandary of inconsistencies for ourselves. What kind of God wills some of us to live in pain while others to live in comfort? If all things come to pass according to God's will, regardless of our choices, action, and inaction, then our free will is a fiction, we are merely pawns, our existence has no meaning, and we have an unfair God. What kind of God wills the holocaust? What kind of God wills his children to live in the squalor of a Jamaican ghetto? What kind of God wills the tortuous death of his own son? This is unthinkable. If we are God's reflection, then clearly the Father could not have willed such misfortunes any more than He could have willed His son's death.

When these misfortunes take place, surely God's grief pales our own. God truly grieves when His children do not do what must be done to bring about His Kingdom, not because He is slighted, but because we are slighted. It is, then appropriate to be thankful for whatever God has provided through his creation (His Providence), but it is arrogant to suppose that God has especially intervened in our situation because of our special merit or prayers or even because of His mercy or that for any reason we are "chosen." This arrogance is particularly pernicious when prayer becomes a petition for God to be on our side in conflict or contest, that our view of the Kingdom becomes God's view. Prayer must not be a veiled complaint about adversity with a request to God that He fix it. Even if we pray that

God's kingdom come, but do nothing but pray, we make mockery of prayer. If we suppose that God intervenes in His creation to spare us misfortune or bring us good fortune, then we can expect to be disappointed with God when misfortune comes our way and we see Him as not intervening. We are indeed "chosen," not to be spared hardships or win some worldly contest, but, rather 2 Thess 2:13: "to be saved through the sanctifying work of the Spirit."

Miracles

The central miracle of Christianity is Christ's resurrection
"And if Christ has not been raised, your faith is futile."
–1 Cor 15:17

A MIRACLE IS NOT A SUSPENSION or violation of natural laws but an event that mirrors God's presence through the response of nature or man to the parameter that is God. A miracle always has a single purpose: to give witness to God. A miracle is characterized by its witness value rather than its presumed inexplicability. A miracle is God's serendipity that reveals His presence. God does not micromanage the universe by intervention, but, with Faith, God is manifest in every present moment which intersects with the eternal, and, thus, every now is a miracle.

Intellectual difficulty with miracles comes from philosophical impediments to accepting the possibility of intervention by God in creation. This is peculiar, since, for everyone, at least one miracle should be self-evident: that is the miracle of creation itself. That the universe exists is a miracle. For Christians, two other miracles are substantive to Christianity itself: the incarnation and the resurrection. Faced with these three monumental miracles, why should we have difficulty with any other event that manifest God? While God relies on His creation and the actions of His children to bring about His kingdom and give witness to His love, God has used the extraordinary to reveal Himself.

It may be true that we often devalue miracles by unwarranted attribution, but that should not compel us to distrust the very possibility and reality of miracles.

Sacrament

A SACRAMENT IS A LITURGICAL symbol or celebration that confers the grace that it signifies. It is an efficacious act that delivers God's grace, because Christ Himself acts in the sacrament. Surely, the most archetypal, and explicit sacrament in Scripture is the Eucharist:

> **John 6:53-58:** Jesus said to them, 'I tell you the truth, unless you eat the flesh of the Son of Man and drink his blood, you have no life in you. Whoever eats my flesh and drinks my blood has eternal life, and I will raise him up at the last day. For my flesh is real food and my blood is real drink.

A sacrament is not a mere metaphor. It is a true mark of God's love and a real seed of His grace, but it is not magic and thus enjoins a response of Faith to convey the life of love that it intrinsically contains.

> **Rom 3:22-24:** ...righteousness from God comes through faith in Jesus Christ to all who believe...and are justified freely by his grace....

Baptism is prominently asserted as sacramental in the Scriptures,

> **1 Pet 3:21:** this water symbolizes baptism that now saves you.... It saves you by the resurrection of Jesus Christ.

In Baptism we are immersed in water that brings both death and life:

> **Rom 6:4:** We were therefore buried with him through baptism into death in order that, just as Christ was raised from the dead through the glory of the Father, we too may live a new life.

This new life is the life of the Word of God and in the sacrament of Baptism this Word is a reality in us,

> **1 Pet 1:23:** For you have been born again, not of perishable seed, but of imperishable, through the living and enduring word of God.

Confirmation has been traditionally practiced since the early Church but has few explicit scriptural references other than references to the laying on of hands. The laying on hands was seen as a source of grace beyond baptism.

> **Acts 8:15-17:** When they arrived, they prayed for them that they might receive the Holy Spirit, because the Holy Spirit had not yet come upon any of them; they had simply been baptized into the name of the Lord Jesus. Then Peter and John placed their hands on them, and they received the Holy Spirit.

The Church recognizes in this the origin of the sacrament of Confirmation, considered to be an affirmation and fullness of baptism in Holy Spirit. Hebrews 6:2 also refers to "instruction about baptisms, the laying on of hands."

Penance is a prerequisite of Christian living, because, although we have been born again in Christ, and, though we have eaten of Christ's body and blood, we are human and as John put it,

> **1 John 1:8 -9:** If we claim to be without sin, we deceive ourselves and the truth is not in us. If we confess our sins, he is faithful and just and will forgive us our sins and purify us from all unrighteousness.

Only God can forgive sins and, as God, He said (Mark 2:5-7) "... your sins are forgiven..." Who can forgive sins but God alone?" The practice of confession developed early in the Church, based on scriptural bidding,

> **John 20:21-23** 'Peace be with you! As the Father has sent me, I am sending you.' And with that he breathed on them and said, 'Receive the Holy Spirit. If you forgive anyone his sins, they are forgiven; if you do not forgive them, they are not forgiven.'

Likewise, Paul refers to the need for reconciliation,

> **2 Cor 5:18-20:** All this is from God, who reconciled us to himself through Christ and gave us the ministry of reconciliation: that God was reconciling the world to himself in Christ, not counting men's sins against them. And he has committed to us the message of reconciliation. We are therefore Christ's ambassadors, as though God were making his appeal through us. We implore you on Christ's behalf: Be reconciled to God.

The bidding to Peter is also recognized in the Church as authorizing

> **Matt 16:18-19:** And I tell you that you are Peter, and on this rock, I will build my church, and the gates of Hades will not overcome it. I will give you the keys of the kingdom of heaven; whatever you bind on earth will be bound in heaven, and whatever you loose on earth will be loosed in heaven.

Holy Orders is seen by the Church as a continuation of the mission entrusted to the apostles by Christ,

> **John 20:21- 22:** Again Jesus said, 'Peace be with you! As the Father has sent me, I am sending you.' And with that he breathed on them and said, 'Receive the Holy Spirit.'

While all the faithful are seen as participating in this priesthood of Christ by virtue of their baptism, confirmation, and the Eucharist, the Church reserves the ministerial priesthood to the episcopacy and presbyterate. Hebrews 5:5-6 tells us, "God said to him, "You are my Son...You are a priest forever, in the order of Melchizedek." Tradition teaches us that this priesthood is passed on through Holy Orders of the apostolic Church. The foundation for this practice is in tradition, with reliance on Judaic practice of the Old Testament, and there are only few and ambiguous references in New Testament Scripture,

> **2 Tim 1:6:** "For this reason I remind you to fan into flame the gift of God, which is in you through the laying on of my hands."
>
> **1 Tim 3:2:** "Now the overseer must be above reproach,"
>
> **1 Tim 3:8:** "Deacons, likewise, are to be men worthy of respect,"
>
> **Titus 1:5-7:** "The reason I left you in Crete was that you might straighten out what was left unfinished and appoint elders in every town, as I directed you. An elder must be blameless, the husband of but one wife, a man whose children believe and are not open to the charge of being wild and disobedient. Since an overseer is entrusted with God's work, he must be blameless..."

Marriage is found throughout human history and is part of Judaic law. As the old covenant was replaced by the new, so also marriage took on new perspective.

> **Matt 19:4-9:** 'Haven't you read,' he replied, 'that at the beginning the Creator made them male and female,' and said, 'For this reason a man will leave his father and mother and be united to his wife, and the two will become one flesh'? So they are no longer two, but one. Therefore, what God has joined together, let man not separate. 'Why then,' they asked, 'did Moses command that a man give his wife a certificate of divorce and send her away?' Jesus replied, 'Moses permitted you to divorce your wives because your hearts were hard. But it was not this way from the beginning. I tell you that anyone who divorces his wife, except for marital unfaithfulness, and marries another woman commits adultery.'

PART 3

VIEWPOINTS

Catholic

BEING CATHOLIC BRINGS an overwhelming sense of humility and confidence. Humility comes from the realization that 2,000 years after Christ, I belong to Christ's historical Church. The Catholic Church of today has an unbroken historical connection to the early Christian Church founded by Christ Himself while He was here and explicitly chose Peter as the first head of His Church

> **Matt 16:18-19:** And I tell you that you are Peter, and on this rock I will build my church, and the gates of Hades will not overcome it. I will give you the keys of the kingdom of heaven; whatever you bind on earth will be bound in heaven, and whatever you loose on earth will be loosed in heaven.

Christ's Church is made up of human beings, and, because of that, suffers many consequent shortcomings, most prominently, divisions. Just as God inspired the meaning of Scripture without suppressing the human character of it, so also Christ inspires and guides His Church through the Holy Spirit without suppressing the human influence. While it is clearly Christ's Will that His people be one:

John 17:22: I have given them the glory that you gave me, that they may be one as we are one.

From its inception the Church has seen disagreements. It was not until Luther, however, that factions of opinions led to major schisms in the Church. Since that time other schisms have taken place and there have been schisms upon schisms, and even fresh reestablishment of Christian churches based on misguided perceptions of God's purpose and an earnest desire to begin anew with an uncontaminated Church.

While there are aspects of the Catholic Church that I consider to be unbalanced, I do not think that God's Will would be served by breaking away and joining some more congenial church or starting my own religion any more than it was served by the history of schisms. Many of the separations took place because the inspirations of the Holy Spirit were not heeded either by the established Church or those seeking to reform or break away from it. Sins of pride on both sides effectively hinder the Holy Spirit.

While there is much that is attractive and useful in Protestant traditions, the separation from the historical Church established by Christ is a fatal flaw. Protestant history goes back only 500 years and has a 1500-year gap to Christ. As the very name "Protestant" implies, it involves protest. If you are protestant, you are opposed, opposed to Catholic, opposed to some other Protestant doctrine, opposed to some authority. This has produced a spectrum of denominations so diverse and conglomerate as to be hardly recognizable as sister churches, running the gamut from fascist fundamentalism to a non-sacramental Christianity that is virtually indistinguishable from a pious humanism. A singular problem, for most Protestants, is opposition to acceptance of the Bishop of Rome as Christ's representative on earth, as the unique authority for Christ on earth.

Many Protestants profess that scripture is the only authority. There is an obvious illogic to this view, since scripture itself does not define which early Christian writings should be taken to be divinely inspired or guided. The compilation of various writings into a single collection we call the Bible is not itself stipulated or even implied in the Bible itself. This very collection, recognized as the sole authority by many, itself relies on human authority in the early Church to identify and define it. Christ did not write any book of the Bible. He did not leave us any writings. He did not create a constitution for His Church. He did not identify a Bible. Instead, He established and organized a central group of disciples, the apostles, to continue and lead His Church, and he selected Peter as the Head.

> **Matt 16:18-19:** ... you are Peter, and on this rock, I will build my church, and the gates of Hades will not overcome it. I will give you the keys of the kingdom of heaven; whatever you bind on earth will be bound in heaven, and whatever you loose on earth will be loosed in heaven.

The early Church was clearly centered on the apostles, and they clearly accepted Peter as their leader. The Catholic Church of today is the evolution of that structure, an apostolic Church with the Bishop of Rome as its leader.

The Essence of Christian Living

SCRIPTURE IS EXPLICIT on what is essential to Christian life:

> **Luke 10:27:** "Love the Lord your God with all your heart and with all your soul and with all your strength and with all your mind'; and, 'Love your neighbor as yourself."
>
> **Gal 5:14:** "The entire law is summed up in a single command: "Love your neighbor as yourself."

Should we have any doubts as to what, specifically, is meant by this, Christ elucidated unambiguously:

> **Matt 25:34-46:** Then the King will say to those on his right, 'Come, you who are blessed by my Father; take your inheritance, the kingdom prepared for you since the creation of the world. For I was hungry and you gave me something to eat, I was thirsty and you gave me something to drink, I was a stranger and you invited me in, I needed clothes and you clothed me, I was sick and you looked after me, I was in prison and you came to visit me.' Then the righteous will answer him, 'Lord, when did we see you hungry and feed you, or thirsty and give you something to drink?

> When did we see you a stranger and invite you in, or needing clothes and clothe you? When did we see you sick or in prison and go to visit you?' The King will reply, 'I tell you the truth, whatever you did for one of the least of these brothers of mine, you did for me.' Then he will say to those on his left, 'Depart from me, you who are cursed, into the eternal fire prepared for the devil and his angels. For I was hungry and you gave me nothing to eat, I was thirsty and you gave me nothing to drink, I was a stranger and you did not invite me in, I needed clothes and you did not clothe me, I was sick and in prison and you did not look after me.' They also will answer, 'Lord, when did we see you hungry or thirsty or a stranger or needing clothes or sick or in prison, and did not help you?' He will reply, 'I tell you the truth, whatever you did not do for one of the least of these, you did not do for me.' Then they will go away to eternal punishment, but the righteous to eternal life.

"Love your neighbor" does not refer to your immediate family, friends, or even the people next door. It refers to all those who are in need and the needy are not just those with whom we would be comfortable. We are called to provide for the needs of people we are likely to find repulsive, contagious, or dangerous. Christ tells us to do this. This is what Christian living is and thus what salvation is all about. This is not a suggestion. It is not an optional matter. Christ says nothing about paying somebody else to do it in our place so that we may remain untouched. He says nothing about praying for these people. He says nothing about going to Church. He says nothing about saying grace. He says nothing about attendance at our Bible study group. He says nothing about doctrines. He says nothing about religious practices or piety. He says nothing about all the admirable, but comfortable, religious activities with which we surround ourselves. There is nothing wrong or objectionable with any of these things; in fact, they are very helpful and supportive of Faith, but they are empty unless we are actively intent on Christ's unambiguous directive. We cannot respond that this is not our calling, that it is for those called to it. We are all called to this by virtue of being called to be Christian.

> **Jas 2:14-17:** What good is it, my brothers, if a man claims to have faith but has no deeds? Can such faith save him? Suppose a brother or sister is

> without clothes and daily food. If one of you says to him, 'Go, I wish you well; keep warm and well fed,' but does nothing about his physical needs, what good is it? In the same way, faith by itself, if it is not accompanied by action, is dead.

Anything that we say or do about Christian living and salvation either confirms what is explicit or implicit in this directive or it obscures it with irrelevance. Unfortunately, it is sadly true that much of religious practice today is so cluttered with pious irrelevance that few Christians recognize Christ's principal directive as pivotal. Christianity is not self-satisfaction derived from doctrinal or emotional fervor. Christian living must remain focused on Christ's core directive. Any religious conviction or fervor without it is an illusion:

> **1 John 4:20-21:** If anyone says, 'I love God,' yet hates his brother, he is a liar. For anyone who does not love his brother, whom he has seen, cannot love God, whom he has not seen. And he has given us this command: Whoever loves God must also love his brother.

Reverence

REVERENCE IS A PROFOUND FEELING of love, awe, and respect for that which is sacred or of God. Reverence is deeply rooted in faith and is an expression of faith. It is not shallow, polite, boring deference or seriousness. Sadly, it is a characteristic of our contemporary materialistic culture to ridicule or condescend reverence. Worse, that which should be revered is often the object of humor that pretends to be harmless, usually at the hands of those who should know better. If an objection is raised, the response is usually, "it was just a joke!" and the one objecting is made to appear humorless. The subject of such humor runs the gamut from God Himself to the Bible, to the Church, to the Sacraments, to the Saints, to Worship, to anything sacred. While humor is healthy and holy, its application to the sacred calls for a level of discernment that all too often fails. The consequences of such humor are not harmless. Not only does it offend those who are sensitive to it, but it also erodes the faith of those who are not.

Dissent

THERE IS INHERENT IN HUMAN politics, including Church politics, a need to control thought. This is especially sinister in the Church when doctrine takes precedence. This is a problem of the human organization, not a problem of truth. It is unfortunate that the Church, be it Catholic or Protestant, places such emphasis on doctrine. Many Protestants insist that the Bible is the only Christian authority, overlooking the inherent inconsistency in that the constitution of the Bible itself requires an external authority. Likewise, in the Catholic Church, there is much emphasis on infallibility. While it is reasonable to assume that God would not allow His Church to misguide His people, does this necessarily have to be in doctrine rather than just the road to salvation? It is true that this cannot be isolated from doctrine, but not all doctrine is equal. Infallibility begs the issue: it says that the Church is infallible because it says that it is. Does this doctrine really matter? Does it impact salvation? Why should salvation be linked to irrelevant doctrines? Does it matter that Mary was assumed into heaven, body and soul? Does it matter if Jesus had siblings? Why should this be a litmus test for anyone?

There is nothing new about all this: even the early Christian Church had problems with attributing importance to the inconsequential, for example, the necessity of circumcision. Even fundamental, but equally mysterious, doctrines such as the trinity should be seen in the perspective of salvation and the core Christian message of love for one's brother. As Matthew 25:31-46 so clearly tells us, at judgment, we will be asked what we did for the "least," who are Christ, not what we think of the trinity. The doctrine of the Trinity is necessary to resolve the appearance of inconsistency between the One God of Judaic tradition and the intractable New Testament references to the Father, Son, and Holy Spirit. The Trinity is necessary, but the New Testament itself leaves it as the mystery which it is, and, perhaps, that is how it should be. The Apostles' Creed is much more comfortable than the Nicene Creed. The penchant of the judicial Church to immerse itself under esoteric scholastic influence, not only in its philosophy and theology, but in its ministering, to define and codify everything from abstinence to venial sin, strains Faith by obscuring focus.

Church bureaucracies too often create volumes of rules and regulations that outdo civil governments. The Code of Canon Law comes close to shaming IRS Regulations. Like civil regulations, Church regulations come with penalties, and Church penalties are usually under pain of sin. The Church should guide and lead the faithful as well as bring those outside the Church to Christ. It cannot do that with rules. It should not compel by edict where it cannot persuade by word or example. Without ever having sacrificed truth, the Church could have averted many a schism by taking a less monarchical stance. The Church must be, above all, a pastoral Church, not a judicial Church.

Conservative elements in the Church often set their defensive position by referring to "cafeteria Catholicism." While this has a valid aspect to it in that arbitrariness is not virtuous, it is more likely true that the displeasing disagreement is about something not essential. It may be about something controversial and emotionally laden, but still not essential to being a true Catholic. Often, the accusation is about some incidental custom. Even then, insecure elements in the Church are often quick to inappropriately remind the offenders of infallibility. There are those in the Church who view honest disagreement as arrogance or as a shortage of humility rather than an honest conscience or intellect or credible ambivalence. They are quick to remind the "dissident" that the Church is not a democracy, which it is not, but fail to appreciate that often the true servant of the Church serves by speaking honestly, possibly as the Holy Spirit inspires, rather than falling in line or mindlessly conforming. The Church is ill served by those who would silence honest dissent or shame honest and conscientious questioning. The Church was not threatened by Galileo's positions, but it was severely injured by those within the Church that silenced him.

More recently, the Pope (ed. John Paul II) has spoken forcibly from conviction and argument against the ordination of women, yet this is not an essential matter to faithfulness and, though the Pope speaks from impressive authority and reasoning, there are many compelling reasons to question the rationale and practice of excluding women from ordination. Likewise, the official Church argues forcibly against contraception and insists that its thinking is the only acceptable position, yet its arguments, based on the natural law, can, using the very same principles of natural law, be honestly and honorably employed to arrive at an opposing position. Again, this is not a question of arrogant pride, but of honest differences. Both positions start from the same premises in natural law, yet honestly and rationally arrive at different conclusions. While these differences may be inconvenient and even upsetting to those less secure, officials in the Church are wrong to insist on submission. Uniformity is not necessarily virtuous and often it is an excuse for laziness, an invitation to smugness, and deprives us of the very truth that we seek to preserve.

Those who lead in the Church need to concentrate on essentials of Faith rather than ambiguous or irrelevant matters. The Church is made up of humans and its bureaucracy (an unfortunate necessity for any large organization of humans) should, after centuries of dealing with correlative truths, dissent, and even heresy, know that belief cannot be compelled and that truth can neither be discovered nor affirmed by edict. The Church, without compromising truth, should be, like Christ, a model of inclusion rather than exclusion. What is essential and what is not? This discernment should come from considering what impact the idea or practice has on the paramount summary of Christianity:

> **Gal 5:14:** The entire law is summed up in a single command: "Love your neighbor as yourself.

Unfortunately, the response of bureaucratic authorities of judicial Church, be it Catholic or Protestant, or even non-Christian, is often to protect its narrow focus by exclusion (formal or informal excommunication).

Fundamentalism

THE GREATEST THREAT TO CHRISTIANITY does not come from its declared enemies. While the Romans feeding Christians to the lions or the intimidations of the godless communist menace were ineffective in accomplishing their purpose, the disposition that Christians share with all religious groups to distort faith into ideology poses a genuine threat to the faith of all.

There is inherent in human nature a need for security. Security is validated by awareness of boundaries and limits. That is the reason why children repeatedly test the limits established by their parents. That is the reason why we have fences. That is likewise the reason why doctrinal purity, that is, ideology, is cherished. People, like water, generally follow the path of least resistance, regardless of where it takes them, which is why they have a dangerous proclivity to focus on rules absolutely without consideration to their intended purpose. The letter of the law is absolute, even if the spirit of the law is contradicted. When doctrinal blindness becomes focused, then terrorism becomes a sanctified and justified reality. In religious context, this is fundamentalism. In political context, it is political correctness. It is a dangerous tendency, particularly for Christians, since it generates self-satisfaction, righteousness, and a presumption of goodness when the rules are being observed, even if compassion and faith are completely absent, and gives issue to an intolerance inconsistent with Christ's message.

The earliest examples of this problem may be found in the early church disagreements about Jewish versus Gentile Christians. Historically, the treatment of Galileo is a well-documented shameful act of the Church. He was fortunate compared to other victims of the inquisitions who paid for their perceived transgressions with torture and death. The Protestant reformation created its own victims. Witch burnings in the New World were not an atypical aberration. Even to this day, righteous ostracism is alive and well. The most scandalous manifestation of this is the incredibly innumerable divisions of Christians, a mutual ostracism. Of course, we also have individual or group condemnations based on the exploitation of Christianity to support personal or group prejudices, such as antisemitism, anti-Catholic, anti-racial, anti-homosexual, or anti whatever one does not like.

Invariably, all these actions arise from a doctrinal disapproval of either expression or action of another Christian or non-Christian person or group. All are a fundamental failure to perceive, or an inability to discern, the applicability of the core Christian message: compassion. Christ came for sinners, not the righteous, for the "least," not the rich. "Let he who is without sin cast the first stone." Those who perpetrate a non-compassionate Christianity in the name of doctrine make a lie of Christianity itself. They are the scribes and pharisees all over again. Defense of doctrinal purity is not an excuse for fundamentally unchristian behavior. If one's action lacks compassion, it is not Christian, regardless of the rhetoric.

These scribes and pharisees are alive and well in most religious institutions and they often focus on doctrinal purity to extremes that lead to contradictions. In many religions, sex is such a focal point. In the Catholic Church, for example, it gives rise to insistence on the perpetual virginity of Mary, because virginity is viewed as superior to non-virginity. There does not seem to be any notice that implies that Mary's and Joseph's marriage was never consummated and thus never truly existed and thus satisfies today's scandalous criteria for annulment. The very concept of "judicial vicar" is a Christian oxymoron. Priests are not allowed to be married in disregard of tradition of the early Church. Peter himself was married. Christ revealed himself in life and after his resurrection first to women, yet Church autocrats close ordination to women. These are human failings in the Church, not Christ's choice.

Death Penalty

MOST, IF NOT ALL, ARGUMENTS in support or against the death penalty ultimately can be reduced to individual perceptions of fairness. Fairness, however, is illusory. Life is fundamentally unfair and any argument centered on it is defeated from the outset. Many are unable to support abolition of the death penalty until the church has a better alternative. It does: Christian forgiveness. True forgiveness (not to be confused with the mushy sentimental stuff of the everybody is OK philosophies!) is the only way to find redemption. Without it, hatred consumes and destroys all victims, including our whole society. The saddest aspect of today's world is the conspicuous absence of redemption in so many places. The death penalty is not so much fair or unfair to the criminal as it is unfair to the rest of us. It deprives the criminal of his life (fairly or not) but deprives us of redemption. Is it worth the price?

APPENDIX

POEMS OF FAITH

My Soul

My soul becoming,
I am who I am.
You dwell within me
as in the Father
and my soul unfolds.
You look upon me,
my soul is boundless.
You gently touch me,
my soul finds fullness.
My soul becoming,
afflicted with fire.
Creation in me,
You softly whisper.
To You, my soul soars.
I am who I am.
I am born, my soul.

WHO ARE YOU?

"Who are you, Lord?" Saul asked. "I am Jesus, whom you are persecuting," he replied.

–Acts 9:5

I am the one who seeks you, my beloved
I am naked and you do not see me
I am in pain and you are confounded
I am much in need and you shy from me
I am a stranger and you reject me
I call to you but you give no answer
I abide with you but you are wary
I hunger and thirst for you without heed
I seek to refresh you but I am spurned
I am the bread of life that you refuse

Bread of Life

I am naked and you do not see me
I am in pain and you are confounded
I am much in need and you shy from me
I am a stranger and you reject me
I call to you but you give no answer
I abide with you but you are wary
I hunger and thirst for you without heed
I seek to refresh you but I am spurned
I am the bread of life that you refuse

Garth

melancholy eyes
compelling abyss of grace
God's own countenance

propitious quiet
arresting revelation
God's own melody

fragile awkward limbs
struggling in outreach of love
God's very own touch

Julian

still unspoken joy
hushed grief of affliction
echo to God's pain

gleam of radiance
smitten by infirmity
mirror to God's love

---

la joie toujours indicible
la peine d'affliction étouffée
écho à la douleur de Dieu

lueur de radiance
frappé par l'infirmité
miroir à l'amour de Dieu

Alone

in the stale shrill of day
blinded by dulling blaze
flaunted and boasted
shouted but unsaid
still unrevealed

in the sad still of night
pressed in by blackness
Everyman a lone star
each a mystery
burning to be found

afflicted shadow of hell
in the company of none
one among many
a sacred miracle
longing for encounter

Acknowledgments

The editor wishes to thank Joy Morin and Stephan Kinsella for constructive editorial and layout suggestions during the assembly of this manuscript.

Resources

The following is a list of articles and books that Leo referenced while writing. It is unclear to what extent the ideas contained in them were incorporated versus being used as more of a source of inspiration during the authoring period. They are provided to the reader for further contemplation.

1. Adler, Mortimer J., editor. "Natural Law." *A Syntopicon of the Great Books of the Western World*, vol. 1, Encyclopædia Britannica, 1952, pp. 450-62.

2. Orwell, George. "A Hanging." *The Collected Essays, Journalism, and Letters of George Orwell*, edited by Sonia Orwell and Ian Angus, vol. 1, Harcourt, Brace & World, 1968, pp. 44-49.

3. "Albert Camus." *Elements of Literature: Sixth Course*, edited by Robert Anderson et al., Holt, Rinehart and Winston, 1997, pp. 1130-32. Was used by: Finstad, Kristina. "Albert Camus." University of New Mexico, 1999, www.unm.edu/~kfinstad/camus.html. *(this URL is defunct now)*

4. Little, Chris. "Bible Supports Death Penalty." *Independence Institute (Independent Feature Syndicate Opinion-Editorial)*, October 29, 1997. Original URL: https://web.archive.org/web/20010217135020/http://i2i.org:80/SuptDocs/OpEdArcv/Op971029.htm Current archived URL: https://web.archive.org/web/20010217135020/http://i2i.org:80/SuptDocs/OpEdArcv/Op971029.htm

5. McKernan, Joe. "God & the Death Penalty." *Plough Online, The Bruderhof Communities*. Original URL, now defunct:

http://www.bruderhof.org/issues/deathpen/thoughts/bible.htm (see Plough.com to request a copy)

6. Schroth, Raymond A., S.J. *Books for Believers: 35 Books That Every Catholic Ought to Read*. Paulist Press, 1987.

7. "Teilhard de Chardin, Pierre." *Twentieth-Century Literary Criticism,* edited by Dennis Poupard, vol. 9, Gale Research, 1983, pp. 476-506.

8. Camus, Albert. "Reflections on the Guillotine." *Resistance, Rebellion, and Death,* translated by Justin O'Brien, Alfred A. Knopf, 1961, pp. 175-234.

9. Linnehan, Paul. "Shadowbrook: Tracking God's Will in a Jesuit Seminary." *The Gettysburg Review*, vol. 11, no. 2, Summer 1998, pp. 253-264.

10. Lukas, Mary, and Ellen Lukas. *Teilhard: The Man, the Priest, the Scientist*. Doubleday, 1977.

Photos

Below is an assortment of photos from Leo's time in Jamaica. It was felt (Ed.) this would provide the reader some context for Leo's experiences there.

Leo (right) with M.O.P founder Fr. Richard Ho Lung

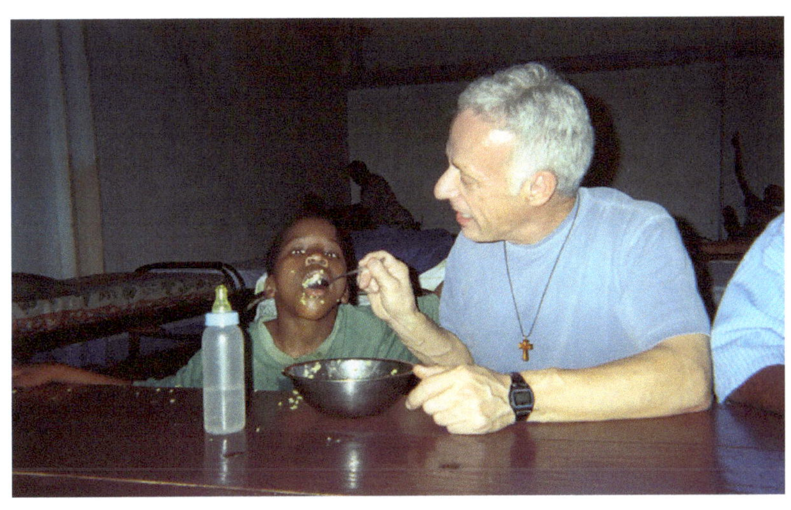

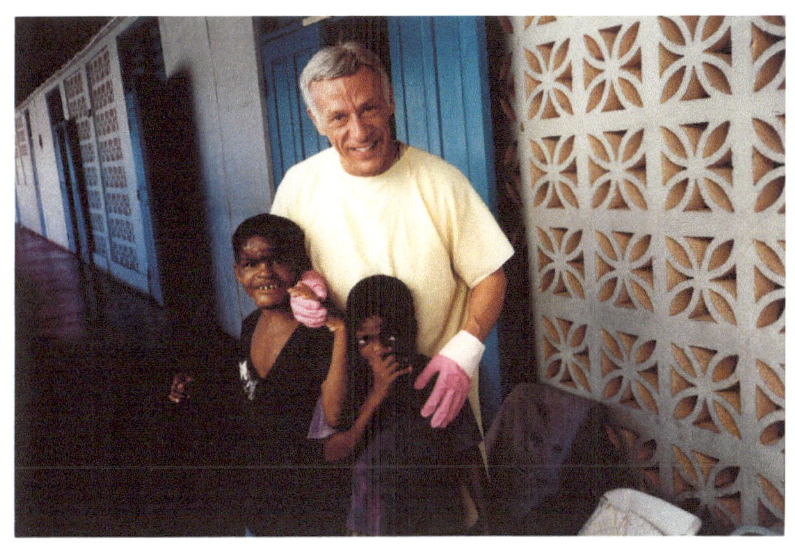

4 25 '99

About the Author

LEO MORIN (1941-2001) WAS BORN and raised in Berlin, New Hampshire, a fiercely Catholic (Guardian Angel Church) and French-Canadian community. He had a natural inclination toward the sciences from an early age, achieving multiple awards at national-level science fairs during high school. Coinciding with his college career (where he pursued degrees in biology and chemistry), he also entered the Jesuit seminary (Shadowbrook in Lenox, Massachusetts). He ultimately left the order after many years and pursued a doctorate in chemistry from Boston College, graduating in 1968. Shortly thereafter, he married, raised three children, and worked in multiple roles, from college professor to Vice President of research and development at several Florida firms. His professional career encompassed dozens of publications and speaking engagements. He and his family eventually moved to Georgia where he pursued a career at the Veterans Administration as a clinical chemist with a simultaneous appointment as Associate Professor of Pathology at Emory University.

His scientific passion for the natural world fed into a love for the hobby of aquarium/fish keeping. His home was peppered with multiple aquariums. This interest eventually led him to start his own company, Seachem Laboratories, Inc., in 1980 in the basement of the family home. Seachem is now a well-regarded worldwide supplier of aquarium products.

Shortly before his untimely death in 2001, he began participating in mission trips to Jamaica under the auspices of his local parish, Corpus Christi in Stone Mountain, Georgia. Those experiences profoundly changed his outlook on life. This book is an outgrowth of those experiences.

www.ingramcontent.com/pod-product-compliance
Lightning Source LLC
LaVergne TN
LVHW052253100826
845147LV00001B/29

* 9 7 9 8 9 9 5 3 6 8 1 2 0 *